FORAGING
IN NORTH AMERICA

THE TOP 12 PLANTS TO SEEK OUT

Anderson

Adventure Skills Guides

IDENTIFY COMMON WILD EDIBLES

Adventure Skills Guides

While there are many excellent guides on foraging, this Adventure Skills Guide is different: It features 12 easy-to-identify plants that are common in most of North America. Ranging from the ubiquitous dandelion to the familiar cattail, the plants included here are easy to identify, abundant, and have a high nutrition value.

If you're a beginning forager, the plants here are a good place to start. By carefully examining the plants you find in the wild—even those you already probably know—you'll hone your observation skills and start to develop the expertise you need to confidently collect for the kitchen table. And once you're ready to get started (and have confirmed your finds), the plants here are simple to gather, and preparing them is easy, whether you're supplementing a recipe or making a main dish. So, get out there, start identifying plants, and enjoy an up-close look at nature's bounty!

TOM ANDERSON

For nearly 30 years, Tom Anderson was a professional naturalist and Director of the Lee and Rose Warner Nature Center near Marine on St. Croix. He is the author of the following titles: *Learning Nature by a Country Road*, *Black Bear: Seasons of the Wild*, and *Things that Bite: The Truth about Critters that Scare People*. He is a native of North Branch, Minnesota.

Cover and book design by Lora Westberg
Edited by Brett Ortler

Cover image: Chudovska/shutterstock.com

All images copyrighted.

Photos courtesy of: Tom Anderson: 3, 18 (inset), 24 (main); Eugene Jercinovic/Public Domain: 20, Hairy-stemmed Spurge; Teresa Marrone: 17

Used under license from Shutterstock.com
13Smile: 4; Angel photographer: 22; : arousa: 18 (main); avoferten: 8 (main); att Benoit: 26; Paul Broadbent: 9; Elena Elisseeva: 5; FJAH: 23; Martin Fowler: 12; Anna Gratys: 14, 27 (bottom); Brian A Jackson: 10; K Hanley CHDPhoto: 6; Przemyslaw Muszynski: 13, 28 (main); nada54: 16; Natali2206: 24, 25; Volodymyr Nikitenko: 21; simona pavan: 14 (main); Zeljko Radojko: 6 (main); Manfred Ruckszio: 11; Elena Rostunova: 28; Ole Schoener: 27 (top); Madeleine Steinbach: 10 (main); tamu 1500: 15; Pavel_Voitukovic: 8; wasanajai: 20 (main); Bertold Werkmann: 19

10 9 8 7 6 5 4

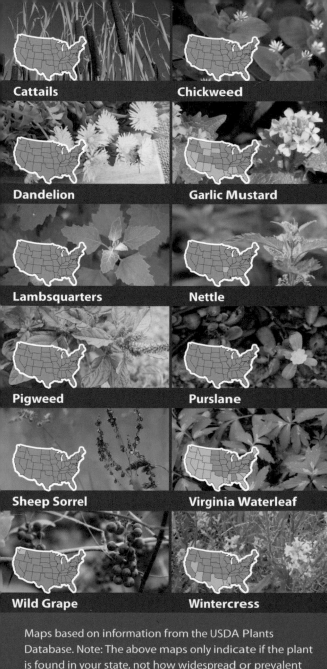

Cattails

Chickweed

Dandelion

Garlic Mustard

Lambsquarters

Nettle

Pigweed

Purslane

Sheep Sorrel

Virginia Waterleaf

Wild Grape

Wintercress

Maps based on information from the USDA Plants Database. Note: The above maps only indicate if the plant is found in your state, not how widespread or prevalent it is. For detailed county-level map information, visit: https://plants.usda.gov/

SOME OF THE AUTHOR'S FAVORITE BOOKS AND WEBSITES:

Dina Falconi's book, *Foraging & Feasting: A Field Guide and Wild Food Cookbook*, is not only filled with excellent recipes, but the illustrations done by Wendy Hollender are a great visual bonus and keen resource.

Leda Meredith's book, *The Forager's Feast: How to Identify, Gather, and Prepare Wild Edibles*, published in 2016 by Countryman Press, is a sumptuous book and an excellent resource.

I am fond of all of Samuel Thayer's books. *The Forager's Harvest, Nature's Garden,* and *Incredible Wild Edibles* are all published by Forager's Harvest Press.

Hank Shaw's books are a treat to look through, and his knowledge and cooking skills are evident. Start with his *Hunt, Gather, Cook: Finding the Forgotten Feast.*

Websites:

Edible Wild Food: www.ediblewildfood.com/foraging-for-food.aspx

Forager's Harvest: www.foragersharvest.com

Botanical Arts Press: www.botanicalartspress.com

For most of human history, wild plants were the mainstay of our diet. Rich in micronutrients (vitamins and minerals) that nurture good health and strong immune systems, the irony is that today many wild plants are demonized. For proof, look no further than the herbicide section of your local hardware store or the common names for many plants, which often include the pejorative word "weed" (e.g., pigweed, chickweed).

This guide is, in part, an attempt to get you to think of wild plants in a different way—as food! The 12 plants featured here are among the top foraging targets, thanks to their accessibility, familiarity, nutritional value, and abundance. Better yet, when compared to cultivated garden plants, wild edibles require far less care, are hardier, and are excellent sources of nutrients.

The plants in this guide also serve as a perfect introduction to foraging, which is fun for the whole family. I encourage you to master these plants and then expand your knowledge with other foraging resources that apply to your region. Before you get started, however, one word of caution: Before eating any wild foods, be sure to confirm that your plant identification is correct. Consulting with several references is a good option, or better yet, go with an experienced forager! If you're not certain, don't eat it!

Once you've confirmed your find, look in the back of this guide for some cooking tips; on the pages that follow, you'll find best practices and ethics on collecting wild foods.

Know What You're Collecting

- Correctly identify the plants you are seeking. There are many good identification tools in print or online. Better yet, join a seasoned forager on an outing.

- Check local resources, such as community education and state and national parks, for foraging classes. These are often a great way to get connected with experts who can help you identify your finds.

- Once you've confirmed your find, eat only a little bit the first few times to see how your system reacts to the new foods.

Collect Legally

- Always obtain permission before foraging if you are not on your own property.

- Be sure you are a legal forager. It may be illegal to forage for plants on public lands. Additionally, be sure the plant you want to collect is not protected in the area you want to forage.

Watch Out for Pollution

- Avoid collecting at the edge of agricultural lands, unless you are certain no toxic herbicides or pesticides have been used. (My garden is a small agricultural land, and we forage there more than anywhere.) Knowing your collecting site is key.

- For obvious reasons, don't collect in an area if dog or cat waste is present. And always wash/rinse foraged items.

- Avoid foraging along roadsides and ditches where vehicles leave a trail of exhaust and other contaminants.

Collecting Ethics

- Refrain from overharvesting. Always leave at least a third of what you find. If you find only a small patch of targeted plants, pass by and let them spread.

- Leave no trace. Don't leave trash. Minimize trampling. Be respectful to the site and to others who might follow.

Practical Tips

- Morning is the best time to harvest. Collect after the dew has dried but before the heat of the day.

- A light pair of gloves can prevent the burn of collecting nettles.

- Be prepared for weather, biting insects, and possible ticks. Sunscreen is also a must in summer.

- Learn to identify poison ivy and poison oak, or your foraging experience could have miserable aftereffects.

- Bring a pocketknife or scissors and a bag, bowl, or basket for carrying your foraged plants.

A Note on Noxious/Invasive Weeds

Some of the weeds in this guide are considered invasive species or noxious weeds in some states because they spread so easily. Before you transplant any of your finds, be sure to check to see if the plant in question is considered noxious in your area: https://plants.usda.gov/java/noxComposite

- Noxious weeds usually must be destroyed to prevent them from spreading. When in doubt, contact your local Extension Service for advice.

CATTAILS
(*Typha* species)

Given their abundance and wide range across North America, cattails are the "supermarket" of the wetland. They can provide a variety of foods for a much longer period of the growing season than most plants. No wild plant can boast of producing more starch (carbohydrates) per acre than cattails.

Habitat Cattails flourish at the shallow edges of wetlands. It is an aquatic plant that emerges well above the water's surface.

Key Identification Characteristics These perennials are capable of growing up to 10 feet tall. The **broad, lance-shaped, dark green leaves** are sometimes several feet long, but not as tall as the flowering stalk.

In late spring and early summer, the top of the cattail stem appears to have two heads. The light green one on top is the male section. Shaped like a skinny hot dog, it produces pollen. The lower one, the female section, is **shaped like a fat hot dog, and it turns velvety brown**. The female section remains into fall, when it fluffs out and disperses its seed.

BEWARE Wild iris (*Iris spp.*) is toxic and has leaves that are shaped like those of cattails. It rarely grows over 3 feet tall, and it often has colorful purple flowers. After it blooms in early summer, the flowering stalk remains and it never has a tall stalk with a cigar-shaped head on top.

Foraging Given that cattails grow in wet places, you will need waterproof boots, hip boots, or waders. Later in the summer, an old pair of tennis shoes may do the trick. Never collect near contaminated waters.

Even though cattail stands tend to be dense, it is a good idea to pull root masses in different locations to minimize the impact, and use a sharp knife to cut the small white shoots from the roots (spring), the main stem (summer), and the thick rhizomes (fall).

Edible Parts

Spring
- Small tapered white shoots growing off the submerged root mass

Summer
- The stem core of the new growth found in the middle of the stem at the base of the plant
- The green flower head (collected well before it releases pollen)
- Pollen

Fall
- Harvest the thick rhizomes after the plant begins to die back.

Preparation In early spring, and again in the fall, gather the tapered white root shoots. These grow like small tusks from the root mass. These can be cooked as a vegetable.

The easiest part of the cattail to eat is the flesh of the basal stalk. This is the portion that grows in the water, just above the mass of starchy roots and to about a foot up the cattail stalk. Peel away the outer leaf sheaths until you get to the tender white core. This can be gently cooked.

When the top (male) cattail head flowers in midsummer, it releases pollen, which is dispersed across the wetland to fertilize other cattails. Bend the plant and insert the cattail head into a paper sack and shake it well. The yellow pollen is nutritious and can be added to pancakes or breads for additional nutrients. It also makes a fine soup thickener.

Early season root shoots, heads, and stalks are all very good in stir-fry dishes. They can also be sautéed or roasted with butter and olive oil.

Steaming the early growth of the male section is super simple. Harvest them before they emerge from their papery sheaths. Slathered with melted butter, you might find yourself giving up corn on the cob. The stalk that runs through the head gives you disposable "cob-holders."

Species Specifics Unlike most wild plants, the green portions of cattails can be harvested from spring through summer.

Because of the plant's high carbohydrate content, plans were underway to feed American soldiers with cattail starch when World War II ended.

Dried cattail leaves are used for making crafts, mats, and baskets.

*Chickweed is a very common plant, and its genus is found around the world. Unfortunately, the second half of its common name contains the word **weed**, and for many people that dooms the plant. I have seen folks on knees in their lawns hunched over patches of chickweed, pulling it and tossing it into a basket to be cast off.*

The genus name of chickweed is Stellaria, a Latin-based name meaning "star." The tiny flowers resemble small, white stars.

Habitat This upland plant has adapted to grow almost everywhere. It has an affinity for rich soils and can be found in lawns, gardens, woods, and woodland edges, and it thrives in shade or sun.

Key Identification Characteristics

- The bright green **leaves are rounded with a distinct tapered point**. They are generally **less than an inch long**.

- Early in the growing season the fragile stems support tiny flower buds covered with fine hairs. Later, **tiny white flowers** will emerge. **Each bloom has five petals, each with two distinct lobes.** (Look closely to see this.)

- It is **low-growing**, only a few inches tall, and can be found in **large expansive mats or patches**. It seems to thrive where the plants support each other.

- Another widespread edible chickweed is Mouse-ear chickweed, which is similar in growth and flowers but has fuzzy stems and leaves. Many sources recommend cooking it before consuming it.

BEWARE Scarlet pimpernel, a toxic look-alike, might be confused with chickweed. It is easy to tell the difference between chickweeds and scarlet pimpernel. Scarlet pimpernel has a hairless, square stem. It has opposite, egg-shaped leaves. The flower is never white and is reddish to scarlet or blue.

Foraging Cool weather in spring is best for finding thick patches of chickweed. The plants usually only last a few months, but, if there is enough moisture and cooler weather, you can harvest them all summer. Due to its fragile, thin stems, it is easy to pick.

I often forage for chickweed for another reason: If I am foraging nettles and carelessly find myself on the burning end of the nettle "sting," I can often find chickweed nearby and make a fresh poultice of chickweed. Directly applying the mashed fresh chickweed on irritated skin can bring some relief.

Edible Parts

- **Leaves and Stems:** Choose the youngest plants, and include the stems and the rich green leaves. While it is best used fresh, harvested chickweed can be refrigerated for a short period of time.

Preparation Eaten alone, chickweed is rather mild. It is best when in the company of other food items. The leaves and thin, tender stems are a great addition to a salad and go nicely with pungent greens, such as dandelion leaves or wintercress.

A favorite dish in our house is a hearty scrambled egg mix that includes a cup of chopped chickweed. It is also a wonderful green to add to your smoothie.

I especially like to eat raw chickweed in wraps and sandwiches. I enjoy sautéing it very briefly in a bit of olive oil to supplement sandwiches, wraps, or burritos. It also serves as a wonderful salad base. I find the subtle flavor of chickweed to resemble corn silk or even corn on the cob.

Species Specifics Chickweed packs a nutritious punch. It has more iron and potassium than any of the domesticated greens. It is packed with vitamins A, C, and D; those from the vitamin B complex; as well as calcium, phosphorus, zinc, manganese, copper, and silica.

It also contains rutin, which helps reduce cholesterol levels, lower blood pressure, and maintains the health of the tiny capillaries in the body.

DANDELION
(Taraxacum officinale)

Dandelion is one of the most recognizable plants in the country, but no plant has been so thoroughly marketed as a "weed." Every spring we are told that the perfect lawn should be dandelion-free. Consequently, weed-killing is big business. I am here to tell you that the much-maligned dandelion is a superfood!

The name dandelion comes from the French dent-de-lion, or lion's tooth, because the dandelion's deeply serrated leaves resemble the sharp teeth of a lion.

Habitat Dandelions thrive almost anywhere that humans go because we disturb the soil. Consequently, lawns, fields, roadsides, vacant lots, and other human-made openings are common places to find dandelions.

Key Identification Characteristics

· In early spring the **rosette of leaves** is easy to identify. **The leaves are dark green, deeply notched, and sharply toothed**.

· The familiar **disc of yellow** is a common, fragrant spring flower. It blooms less profusely in the summer. When the flower goes to seed, the **delicate ball of fluff** is equally familiar. Under the right conditions, these seeds can be dispersed for miles.

Foraging

· Tear the leaves from the plant.

· Young leaves and those from plants growing in shade are less bitter.

- When collecting flowers, gather them when the bloom is at its peak.

- Roots are best collected from second-year plants and should be dug up after September. This way the roots will be firm and have all the nutrients in them.

Edible Parts

- **Leaves:** Fresh in salads, sandwiches, and wraps or sautéed in olive oil.

- **Flowers and buds:** Dandelion blossoms and buds add edible color to a salad and are used to make wine.

- **Flower stems:** The stalks can be boiled up as a substitute for traditional spaghetti noodles.

- **Taproot:** The roots can be roasted for a dandelion coffee.

Preparation Mixing dandelions with spinach or lettuce adds a peppery flavor to those blander greens while adding tons of nutrients. (Iceberg lettuce, the most popular, cheapest, and nutrient-poor of the lettuces, has only a fraction of the total nutrients and minerals of dandelion greens!)

To minimize bitterness, particularly when eating them raw in a salad, add balsamic vinegar; a little sugar or honey, or fats, such as butter, bacon grease, or oils.

A third way to reduce or eliminate the bitterness is to boil the greens for 3–5 minutes, change the water, and then boil them again for the same amount of time.

Species Specifics Compared to spinach, dandelion leaves have eight times more antioxidants, two times more calcium, more vitamin A, and nearly two times more vitamin K and vitamin E. They are also a good source of vitamin B6, thiamine, riboflavin, potassium, copper, magnesium, and manganese.

Adding dandelions to your diet may reduce the risk of cancer. They are high in vitamin C and luteolin, which reduce free radicals (major cancer-causing agents) in the body.

Garlic mustard is an invasive species. Brought to North America from Europe for food and medicine, it has spread to 27 states and is considered noxious because it quickly takes over the forest floor and can overwhelm native woodland flowers. Worse yet, it spreads easily, as the small prolific seeds stick to shoes or the feet of wildlife and can accidentally spread to new growing sites. Happily, there's an easy way to fight back: eat it!

Habitat Garlic mustard grows best in full to partial shade and is most commonly found in wooded areas.

Key Identification Characteristics

- The **deep green leaves are rounded, with a heart or kidney shape**. They appear slightly wrinkled and are **scalloped along the edges**. The easiest way to identify garlic mustard is to **crush the leaves and smell the distinct garlic or onion aroma**.

- This biennial ranges from 1–4 feet tall. Its numerous small, **rounded clusters of white flowers** grow only in its second year. Each flower has **four distinct petals**.

- The flowers of the second-year plant will develop into slender 2-inch seedpods. One garlic mustard plant can produce 8,000 seeds!

Foraging Collect leaves from this plant from early spring to June. Leaves growing in shade are most flavorful. Older leaves tend to be more bitter, especially during the hot summer months.

Given how prolific and invasive this plant is, it is a good idea to pull the entire plant out of the ground and strip the leaves for food.

The roots can be gathered at any time. These can be minced very finely in a food processor for a horseradish substitute.

The tiny black seeds can be gathered by stripping dry pods into a plastic bag later in the summer. Crumple the bag to free the seeds, and then pull out as much of the dried stem and leaf pieces (chaff) as you can. Use a fan to separate the rest of the chaff. It is a good idea to spread a tarp under your working area to collect chaff and spilled seed. You want to avoid spreading the seeds.

Edible Parts

- **Leaves** are best harvested in spring when they are most tender.
- The **flowering stalks** resemble the loosely flowered heads of broccoli. Gather them when they are young and tender, just before the flowering heads open.
- **Roots** can be harvested anytime.
- Gather **seed** after the seedpod dries.

Preparation One of my favorite methods to prepare the leaves is to make and freeze lots of pesto. With its already garlicky taste, you can reduce the amount of garlic usually used in your favorite pesto recipe.

The tender flowering stalks can be quite bitter, so blanch them for 3–4 minutes to help reduce bitterness. Then sauté them in olive oil and some minced garlic for about a minute. Add grated Parmesan cheese and lemon zest for a treat.

Shredded leaves are a great addition to salads, wraps, scrambled eggs, rice, quinoa, or mashed potatoes. As the leaves of raw garlic mustard contain small amounts of cyanide, giving it its bitter taste; consuming small amounts of raw leaves on an occasional basis is best. Cooking eliminates the problem.

Garlic mustard seeds can be ground to make a coarse-ground mustard.

Species Specifics Its abundance in some areas makes for bountiful harvesting. You can feel good about using it freely because it is an invasive.

The greens of this plant harbor nutritious amounts of vitamins A, C, E, and some of the B vitamins. It is a good source of minerals, such as calcium, potassium, magnesium, iron, and more. It is a source of Omega-3 fatty acids.

This plant was introduced to North America by European settlers and is one of the easiest plants to find. A prodigious seed producer, most vegetable gardeners consider lambquarters a weed, as it is found nearly everywhere. But there's good news: Also known as "wild spinach," lambquarters offers more nutrients and delivers more protein than supermarket spinach. Still, this is one of those wild edibles that can be too much of a good thing. Eat it or weed it before it goes to seed.

Habitat Lambsquarters is ubiquitous and lives in a wide range of habitats. It does especially well in vegetable and flower gardens, fallow fields, and other disturbed ground. With full sun, it can grow almost anywhere.

Key Identification Characteristics

- The upper surface of the green leaves, particularly near **the tip, looks like the plant has been lightly sprinkled with talcum powder**. This is due to a white, waxy-coating of tiny crystals on the leaf surface. The thick stem also has the pale dusty coating. Test it by rubbing it off with your fingers.

- The **bluish-green leaves are broadly toothed**, resembling a spear or a narrow goose's foot.

- As it grows taller, sometimes up to 5 feet tall, it develops clusters of very small, greenish flowers.

BEWARE Nightshade is a poisonous plant that looks kind of like lambquarters, but it never gets the white waxy dusting and does not get as tall.

Compared to the tiny green inflorescence at the tip of a lambsquarters plant, nightshade's larger, bell-shaped, colorful flowers grow scattered along its branches. The flowers of nightshade become shiny black or red pea-sized berries. There are no berries on lambsquarters.

Foraging Lambsquarters is a great plant to teach to children as it is extremely common and easy to identify.

For fresh greens, it is best to harvest the young lambquarters that are no taller than 6 inches. When the stem gets taller, thicker, and more fibrous, simply pinch or snip the upper leaves. Those leaves at the top of the plant are newest and most tender.

Edible Parts

- **Tender leaves** from young plants are preferred.
- **Seeds** are easy to plant/sprout for use as micro-greens.

Preparation Mix fresh leaves in a salad, smoothie, or with sandwich greens. As in spinach, oxalic acid is found in raw lambsquarters leaves. Oxalic acid can interfere with the absorption of calcium, but its benefits far outweigh the negatives. Oxalic acid is broken down in cooking, and it doesn't hinder the absorption of calcium from other foods.

Lightly steam or sauté fresh leaf greens. Be sure to gather about twice as much as you think you need, as they will reduce while cooking.

Garnish with a splash of lime or lemon juice. This is a great addition to rice, quinoa, or even yogurt.

Species Specifics The deep taproot has the ability to pull up nutrients from the subsoil, so be sure there are not contaminants in the soil where you forage.

One cup of greens contains approximately 73 percent of the recommended daily allowance of vitamin A and nearly 96 percent of the recommended daily intake of vitamin C.

It is a great source of the B vitamins, including niacin, riboflavin, and thiamine.

NETTLE
(Urtica dioica)

This plant is known as "itchweed" because of the stinging hairs found on the stems and leaves. These contain histamine and other chemicals that cause a temporary burning pain. The long, hollow hairs have evolved as an adaptation to keep herbivores from eating the plant. Unlike an experience with poison ivy, the "burn" of a nettle encounter is short-lived and disappears within a couple of hours. But once cooked or dried, the stinging property disappears, and the plant becomes a wonderful green chock-full of vitamins, nutrients, and flavor.

Habitat Nettles thrive in a wide range of habitats. They are most abundant in full sun or partial shade. You can find them along roadsides, edges of wetlands, gardens, and almost anywhere the soil has been disturbed, allowing the tiny seeds to germinate.

Its large root mass can also spread vegetatively (via spreading roots).

Key Identification Characteristics

- The **dark green leaves, 3–6 inches long, are coarsely toothed and grow in opposite pairs. The veins on the mostly hairless upper surface of the leaves are sunken, while they are raised on the underside**. The small **stinging hairs** are found on the surface of the leaves and are orientated toward the leaf tip. Those found on the stem are more conspicuous.

- **Spikes and clusters of tiny greenish flowers grow at the tip of the plant and in the leaf axils**.

- Nettles can grow to 6 feet tall but are best used when 6–12 inches tall.

BEWARE White snakeroot is toxic to cattle and humans, but there are a number of ways to differentiate it from stinging nettle. It tends to prefer shady areas rather than openings. Its leaves are also slender and toothed, but they are mostly smooth and **bear no hairs**. The **stem is also hairless. The lower leaves are heart-shaped**. White snakeroot bears clusters of **small white flowers, not green**, in late summer and early fall.

Another look-alike is wood nettle, which is most commonly found in large, expansive patches in low floodplain areas and tends to prefer shade. As with stinging nettle, wood nettle can cause discomfort if you rub against it.

Its leaves are oval-shaped and are broad, rather than slender. It does not grow nearly as tall as stinging nettle. Some foragers consider them superior in taste to stinging nettles. They are also nutrient and vitamin rich. But they also **must** be cooked before eating.

Foraging Look for this plant early in the spring; harvest the tender growth when it is less than a foot tall. Older, taller plants are more fibrous.

To prevent discomfort from the stinging hairs, use gloves and scissors when harvesting.

Edible Parts

- In the spring, with early growth, you can harvest the entire exposed **plant**. Later, as the plant grows taller, I harvest the newest leaves found at the tips.

- **Avoid** harvesting plants that are in flower or very tall. Older leaves are gritty due to microscopic calcium crystals, and these can cause kidney problems.

- Collecting **leaves** to dry for a tea can be done during any time in the growing season.

Preparation Boiling, steaming, or sautéing nettles nullifies the painful itch. Never eat them raw.

I mostly use nettles by sautéing them in a little hot olive oil until they just start to turn crispy. I add them to sandwiches or burritos, or eat the cooked leaves as chips.

Raw leaves can be cooked directly in a pizza, lasagna, soup, or egg dish.

Species Specifics Nettles contain more protein per ounce than any other edible leafy green plant!

Nettles are among the best plant sources of iron. They harbor a host of beneficial minerals, such as phosphorous, sulfur, manganese, potassium, and calcium.

The common name of this plant isn't exactly appealing. Other names, such as wild amaranth, green amaranth, and redroot amaranth, are more inviting. Sadly, once you tag a plant with the suffix "weed," most folks want to declare war on it rather than consider its virtues as a fine, edible plant. In the plant world, you need to hang your judgment at the door.

Habitat This annual thrives in disturbed sites, abandoned fields, and almost anywhere humans are found. Pigweed can withstand a tough life of heat, drought, and general abuse.

Key Identification Characteristics

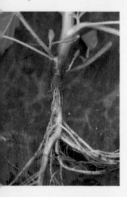

- The easiest identification marker is the **red-purple color at the base of the stout stem**; this coloration is also found in the taproot.

- The **slightly droopy leaves** can grow up to 5 inches long and are **egg- to diamond-shaped**. They grow alternately from each other and are slightly hairy on the under side while being smooth on top.

- The foliage branches thickly off the main stem of mature plants, giving them **a bushy aspect**. Pigweed is capable of growing up to 6 feet tall.

- Dense, short hairs are found at the top of the stem.

- Later in the summer, the plant has large, erect spikes of tiny **bunched, nondescript, greenish flowers growing at the tip** of the plant or in the axils.

BEWARE Deadly nightshade and bitter-sweet nightshade might be confused with pigweed, but a quick inspection will show them to be quite different. Nightshades have distinctive *bell-shaped* flowers growing off the branched stems. Each bloom is roughly an inch long and greenish to purple in color. The pea-size shiny black and red berries make it easy to avoid, as none of the wild amaranths grow berries.

Foraging Pigweed leaves are tastiest in the spring and early summer, when they are young.

In late summer or early fall, the brown-to-black, very tiny seeds are abundant and easy to strip off the plant. Cut the seed-bearing branches and beat them on a clean white sheet to dislodge the seeds. It is important to use a large sheet to capture the seeds. As the plant can become invasive in some areas, it is necessary to contain them. Use a fan, set a few feet away, or the wind to winnow the chaff from the seed. If the seeds are dry and kept in an air-tight container, they will keep for a long time.

Edible Parts

- Seek out **young leaves**, in spring and early summer. **Older leaves** are also edible but require cooking.
- Harvest **seeds** later in the summer.

Preparation Young pigweed leaves can be added raw to a salad. Older leaves should be cooked as you would prepare spinach or other greens. You can pickle, can, freeze, or dry leaves for winter use. Leaves must be blanched before freezing.

The seeds can be eaten raw, parched, or roasted in the oven. They can be ground and used as a flour, soup thickener, or hot cereal.

Species Specifics Pigweed is loaded with iron and other minerals, such as calcium and phosphorous. It also contains vitamins A and C and is high in fiber. Amaranth seeds are an amazing 12–17 percent protein.

Note: Some pigweed species, such as Palmer amaranth *(Amaranth palmeri)* and common waterhemp *(Amaranth rudis)* are prohibited noxious weeds in many states and must be destroyed. They are relatively easy to tell apart from the pigweed species shown here, as the noxious species have **hairless stems**. They also lack the red root of *Amaranthus retroflexus*.

Purslane is another tenacious dweller of gardens. This native of India and Iran is extremely persistent and has spread throughout the world as an edible plant, as well as a plant that gets in the way of gardeners. Harvest it for the table rather than toss it on a weed pile. This low, creeping plant was valued for thousands of years in the Old World. Recently folks in North America have begun realizing its nutritional value.

Habitat Like most so-called weeds, this plant grows very well on disturbed ground, such as in gardens. It grows equally well on fertile or dry, poor soil. Its succulent nature makes it very drought tolerant.

Purslane seeds germinate best in warm soil. This means it appears later in the growing season than early spring greens.

Key Identification Characteristics

· Purslane has **fleshy, succulent, rounded leaves**.

· The leaves and **small yellow flowers** are found on its **thick reddish-green stems**.

· The reddish-green **stems spread out on the ground like miniature hoses** over a single taproot. A large plant can **resemble a mat of leaves**.

BEWARE Spurges are a group of toxic plants that resemble purslane in the manner they grow and spread close to the ground. However, a close look reveals that a spurge's leaves are *not succulent and thick*. Instead, they are paper thin and are slightly toothed, unlike the smooth edge

Hairy-stemmed Spurge

of purslane leaves. The key difference is the sap in their stems. Spurges have *milky sap or latex* instead of the clear sap found in purslane.

Foraging Given how often it grows on disturbed ground such as a garden or yard, this plant is one of the easiest plants to forage.

Because it hugs the ground like a carpet, it needs to be rinsed well to remove any soil or grit.

Edible Parts

- Veteran foragers prefer the **young leaves** and the **tender tips of the stem**.
- Do not waste time plucking individual small leaves off the plant. Instead cut segments off of the stem.
- The **buds and flowers** are also tasty.

Preparation I find that the tender stems and leaves found growing at the tips of the plant have a taste similar to spinach. Overall, it is mild tasting. Nutritionally, it is best eaten raw. Try it in salads, smoothies, and sandwiches.

If you cook it, sauté it or lightly steam it. It is a good substitute for spinach.

Species Specifics Purslane has been used as a vegetable and medicinal plant for more than 4,000 years. This leafy green has crazy amounts of vitamin A, which is an excellent antioxidant; vitamin A also has benefits for vision and can may lower the risk of certain types of cancer. Purslane has high levels of iron and potassium too. This green is rich in Omega-3 fatty acids; it has five times more than spinach, making it very heart-healthy.

Recent research has also found that purslane has higher nutritional value than most cultivated vegetables and boasts higher levels of vitamin A, ascorbic acid, and alpha-linolenic acid.

SHEEP SORREL
(Rumex acetosella)

If I need a tasty pick-me-up in the garden, I'll search out this perennial. A few fresh sheep sorrel leaves provide a little kick of a sour-apple taste. While not a true grass, an old common name for it is "sour grass." That characteristic makes this plant a fun one to pick and nibble with kids. They love the delightfully tart taste. While other plants in the buckwheat family tend to be knee to waist high, this one is short and somewhat fragile.

Habitat It thrives in disturbed sites, abandoned fields, roadsides, and almost anywhere humans are found.

Key Identification Characteristics

- Leaves: In spring and early summer, only the basal clump (rosette) of leaves is found. **The leaves have a distinct arrow shape** to them, with a flare at the base of the leaf.

- In summer, **the 4- to 15-inch-tall flowering stalk develops. It is smooth and reddish.** Each is graced with tiny green, yellow, or red flowers. Each flower will give rise to a single seed that is wrapped in a somewhat translucent covering.

- Plants are often found in large colonies due to the spread of rhizomes. This plant may frustrate gardeners because their hoeing only breaks up the rhizomes, creating more plants.

Foraging Collect the leaves. Larger leaves are best, 1½–2 inches in length, as they are simpler to collect and will fill your basket more quickly. Unlike other wild greens that grow bitter with age, sheep sorrel can be harvested from spring through fall.

Edible Parts

- **Leaves** are the only part used for food. It's always fun to watch someone sample this plant, as it has a very distinct tartness to it.

Preparation Because this plant shrinks so much when it is cooked, it is generally not cooked as a green. Doing so requires too much work and not much to show for it.

Because it is packed with a pleasing tartness, a handful of fresh leaves are a great addition to soups, salads, and sandwiches.

Drying it will give you another secret ingredient when cooking up a favorite winter soup.

The tartness of the plant makes it a great trail snack.

Given that sheep sorrel contains oxalic acid, it's a good idea not to overload yourself with too much sorrel at one sitting. Oxalic acid is often portrayed as a dangerous component, but many foods purchased at your grocery store contain oxalic acid and there are no warnings on them. With that said, if you are concerned about certain health issues, such as kidney stones or gout, be sure to consult with your doctor before consuming it.

Species Specifics This ubiquitous plant is a rich source of vitamins C, E, and beta-carotenoids. Some herbalists consider sheep sorrel to be one of the most potent sources of antioxidants.

This native woodland plant is easy to recognize and lovely when flowering. Virginia waterleaf colonized the perimeter of my yard after I accidentally brought it in while transplanting a tree from some nearby woods. This lovely perennial, also known as Shawnee Salad, has become a welcome green to add to our spring and summer cuisine.

Habitat Virginia waterleaf prefers shade or partial sun and tends to flourish in rich woods or floodplains.

Key Identification Characteristics

- In the spring, this plant is easily identified by the **scattering of white spots on the green leaf**. Resembling water stains, this feature gives them their common name. By summer the white markings disappear and the plants are uniformly green.

- **The leaves, measuring up to 6 inches long and 4 inches across, have coarsely toothed edges with a sharp tip**.

- From April to June, the waterleaf blooms. The flowers vary in color from pink to light violet to white and are **quite showy with pronounced long, hairy stamens**. Each plant generally has one or two flower clusters, each perched on a naked stalk.

- The plant stands 1 to 2 feet tall, with a somewhat weak stem that is sometimes slightly hairy.

Foraging Gather young leaves, as they are less fuzzy and more tender than older ones. Even though waterleaf can be abundant, it is best to collect only one leaf per plant so as to minimize stress to the plant.

Edible Parts

- **Spring leaves**, gathered before the flowers emerge, are delicious raw. After flowering, the leaves become more bitter, but they are good when cooked as greens.

Preparation Young leaves are a tasty treat as you stroll through the woods. These same leaves are a good addition to salads. They can be sautéed as a cooked green.

When cooking more-mature leaves, it is recommended to boil them for 3 minutes, drain the water, and boil the leaves a second time for 3–5 minutes. I like to toss the cooked greens with some olive oil and a splash of lemon or lime juice.

Species Specifics This plant is usually abundant when you find a patch, so gathering it is easy. A thorough analysis of the nutritional values is lacking, but it is known to be a source for vitamins A, C, and E.

Waterleaf flowers are especially attractive to a number of pollinators, such as bumblebees, small carpenter bees, and other long-tongued bees. The native waterleaf cuckoo bee feeds *only* on plants in this genus.

Just as cuckoo birds lay their eggs in another bird's nest, the cuckoo bee will leave an egg in another bee's nest. The cuckoo larvae hatch first and then eat the other bees' pollen provision.

WILD GRAPE
(Vitis species)

Roughly 20 species of wild grapes live in North America. Wild grape is a vine that must climb something rigid, like trees, fences, or walls, to reach sunshine. The vine can climb to the tops of trees and reach more than 30 feet in height.

Habitat Sunny locations, such as the south-facing side of a clearing, riverbank, or woods. It may also cover brush piles and fence lines.

Key Identification Characteristics

- This woody vine has no stem or trunk. Larger specimens can be 2-4 inches thick near the base. **The thin brown bark on the main vine is shaggy**.

- As it climbs, the vine's girth lessens, and it sprouts smaller vines along its length. These branch onto anything that the **grasping tendrils** can wrap around.

- **The bright green leaves are deeply lobed, coarsely toothed, and heart-shaped**. The non-woody tendrils are typically opposite the leaf.

- **Small white flowers** appear in early summer and grow in clusters that hang nearly 4 inches long.

- In the fall, many bunches of grapes can be found on one vine. Each bunch cluster usually contains 10-20 fruits. The fruits range in color from purple to dark blue to almost black. **They are often covered with a whitish blush**. This is a fine layer of harmless waxy substance that serves to protect the fruit.

Foraging Leaves are best in late spring and early summer when they are tender. I prefer those growing near the tip of the vine, as they are youngest and most tender.

Grapes ripen in late summer and early fall. My great-uncle always said that grapes taste sweeter when their "hides have been nipped by a frost." It's true. Snack on them right off the vine or collect them in a container to bring home.

> **BEWARE** There are two species of wild plants, Canada moonseed and Virginia creeper, that might be confused with wild grape. Both are **toxic**.
>
> *Differences between Canada moonseed and wild grape:*
>
> - Canada **moonseed vines have no tendrils**. Wild grape has many tendrils.
>
> - Canada **moonseed fruits have one seed** that is crescent-shaped (like a crescent moon). Wild grapes have many small, round seeds.
>
> - Moonseed leaves **are not toothed** and are more rounded than the sharper leaves of wild grape.

> *Differences between Virginia creeper and wild grape:*
>
> - Virginia creeper leaves are slightly toothed, like those of wild grape, but they **are not lobed**.
>
> - Virginia creeper usually has **five leaflets that grow palmately**, like spokes growing off a hub, unlike wild grape leaves that arise singly off the vine.
>
> - The stemlets **that bear the purple fruit are distinctly red**.

Preparation Small, tender wild grape leaves are wonderful as an addition to a salad or when sautéed in olive oil.

The leaves can be canned, pickled, or blanched and frozen.

Grape juice makes excellent jellies and syrups. Because of its tartness, you need to add sugar. It is a good idea to wear rubber gloves when processing berries to juice, as the naturally occurring tartaric acid can irritate your skin.

Species Specifics Wild grapes are a good source of vitamins A, C, E, K, and many B vitamins. Minerals include iron, calcium, potassium, and magnesium.

Grapes are a rich source of resveratrol, part of a group of compounds called polyphenols. Resveratrol is being studied for its potential to decrease the risk of heart disease and cancer.

WINTERCRESS
(Barbarea vulgaris)

As winter's snow melts away, one of the first splashes of green you'll see are the ground-hugging basal leaves of wintercress. This member of the mustard family is hardy and can survive winter under a blanket of snow.

Later on in the spring, the shin-high bright yellow flowers are testimony to another common name, yellow rocket.

Habitat Wintercress is a biennial that prefers disturbed soil, and it is found along fields, roadsides, in lawns, and on construction sites.

Key Identification Characteristics

- **In its first year, only the basal leaves appear**; in its second year, the plant will flower.

- The leaves at the base of the first-year plant are up to 6 inches long and nearly 3 inches across. They are lobed, with a large, rounded tip.

- **The yellow flowers of the second-year plant grow in clusters at the tip of the flowering stalk**. The flower clusters are 1-1½ inches across. Each individual flower within the cluster is about a third of an inch across and is made up of **4 yellow petals**.

- **Leaves growing on the stem are much smaller than the basal leaves and appear to hug or clasp the stalk**.

- There can be several hairless stems coming from the base of leaves that give the plant the appearance of a clump. **The stems often have purple streaks or stripes**.

- In late spring and summer, slender green seedpods, measuring an inch or so in length, grow off the stem. Each pod contains hundreds of tiny brown seeds.

Foraging The best time to forage and eat the raw, dark green, shiny leaves is in early spring before the flowering stalk emerges. The leaves and flower buds can be consumed all summer.

Additionally, this is one of the rare plants that you can forage in the winter if your winters are not too severe. Dig down through the snow in areas where you have gathered the plant in spring and summer and you will find green leaves ready to collect. This winter hardiness, and the plant's vitamin C levels, made it invaluable in the days when scurvy was a concern.

Edible Parts

- **Leaves**, particularly the larger basal leaves
- **Flower buds and flower heads** of the second-year plant
- **Seeds**

Preparation Freshly picked leaves added to a salad or sandwich offer a distinct peppery taste.

Cooking wintercress makes it less pungent and peppery.

Seeds can be ground for homemade mustard.

I like this tasty dish: Snip the flowers just below the buds and add them and some wintercress greens to boiling water. Cook for 2-3 minutes. Drain the water off, rinse them with cold water, and taste. If it's too bitter for your palate, repeat with another boiling. After draining the water off, I like to add some butter or olive oil with a dash of lime or lemon juice.

Species Specifics This plant has a crazy amount of vitamin A. Rich in vitamin C, it was commonly cooked in previous centuries to prevent scurvy, a horrible disease resulting from the lack of vitamin C. It is also a good source of minerals, such as calcium, potassium, phosphorous, and iron.

Note: Wintercress is a noxious plant in some states. Before you transplant or harvest it, check here to get information for your state: https://plants.usda.gov/java/noxComposite

These are two recipes that you can use for plants with edible greens.

Foraged Greens Sauté

- Sauté a chopped garlic clove in a tablespoon of olive oil in a shallow pan or a frying pan.

- After a minute, add a bulky handful of loosely chopped greens and a tablespoon of water.

- Cover and cook on low heat for 4–5 minutes.

- Remove the cover and add a dash of balsamic vinegar or fresh lemon or lime juice.

- Cook, uncovered, until the leaves have fully wilted. Enjoy!

Foraged Greens Pesto

- 6 cups fresh foraged greens (my favorites are dandelion, chickweed, lambsquarters, and garlic mustard)

- 5–10 cloves of garlic (depending on size and intensity of garlic clove and your personal taste)

- 1 cup olive oil

- 1 tablespoon sea salt

- 1 cup walnuts, sunflower seeds, or pine nuts

- Zest from 1 lemon (I recommend organic because you are using the skin)

Directions Harvest greens with knife or scissors to avoid dirt. Rinse and dry. In a food processor, blend garlic cloves with a few tablespoons of the olive oil.

Add greens, salt, nuts, and zest to a food processor; pulse until mixture becomes a thick spread. Some people like their pesto chunkier, while others like it super smooth. This is a matter of personal choice.

Eat fresh on noodles, sandwiches, eggs, pizza, crackers, or vegetables.

Store in refrigerator for up to two weeks. Freezing pesto can be convenient in ice-cube trays. Empty pesto cubes into zip-lock bags so that you can defrost just the right amount.

GLOSSARY

Alternate leaves: Leaves not directly opposite each other but alternating along the stem or points of growth

Opposite leaves: Leaves situated directly opposite each other from their point of growth

Annual: A plant that completes its life cycle in one year and then dies

Axils: The angle at the junction of two parts of the plant, such as the junction of the leaf and the stem or stalk

Basal leaves: Leaves that arise from the root stalk rather than the stem; they appear to lay on the ground

Biennial: A plant with a two-year life cycle

Entire leaves: Leaves with a continuous, unbroken margin or edge

Lobed leaves: Leaves with distinct protrusions that are pointed or rounded

Petiole: The stalk-like portion of a leaf

Palmate: With three or more leaflets or branches growing from one point; similar to spokes connected to a hub

Perennial: Living several years

Rhizome: An underground root stalk that grows horizontally and creates new plants

Rosette: A dense circular cluster of leaves

Serrated leaves: Bearing teeth along the edge of the leaves

Simple leaves: A singular leaf (of which there are many shapes)

Stamens: The male or pollen-producing organ of the flower

Succulent: Having thick, fleshy stems; these are adaptations for water storage and are found more commonly on plants thriving in hot or dry environments

Tendril: A thin twisting, clinging offshoot, a mini-vine of sorts, which enables a vine to attach itself to another object or another plant for support

Safely Gather These Widely Accessible Plants

Learn to identify, collect, and prepare wild edibles!

Simple and convenient—harvest an abundance of free, nutritious plants

- Pocket-sized format—easier than laminated foldouts

- Professional photos and expert tips for positive ID

- Easy-to-use information for even beginner foragers

- Advice to help you avoid toxic or inedible look-alikes

- Author's best practices, based on 30 years of experience

Collect all the Adventure Skills Guides

SPORTS & RECREATION/OUTDOOR SKILLS/FORAGING

ISBN 978-1-59193-832-3   **$9.95**

50995

9 781591 938323